1935 i... read a good book, you needed either a lot of money or a library card. Cheap paperbacks were available, but their poor production generally mirrored the quality between the covers. One weekend that year, Allen Lane, Managing Director of The Bodley Head, having spent the weekend visiting Agatha Christie, found himself on a platform at Exeter station trying to find something to read for his journey back to London. He was appalled by the quality of the material he had to choose from. Everything that Allen Lane achieved from that day until his death in 1970 was based on a passionate belief in the existence of 'a vast reading public for *intelligent* books at a low price'. The result of his momentous vision was the birth not only of Penguin, but of the 'paperback revolution'. Quality writing became available for the price of a packet of cigarettes, literature became a mass medium for the first time, a nation of book-borrowers became a nation of book-buyers – and the very concept of book publishing was changed for ever. Those founding principles – of quality and value, with an overarching belief in the fundamental importance of reading – have guided everything the company has done since 1935. Sir Allen Lane's pioneering spirit is still very much alive at Penguin in 2005. Here's to the next 70 years!

# MORE THAN A BUSINESS

'We decided it was time to end the almost customary half-hearted manner in which cheap editions were produced – as though the only people who could possibly want cheap editions must belong to a lower order of intelligence. We, however, believed in the existence in this country of a vast reading public for intelligent books at a low price, and staked everything on it'
**Sir Allen Lane, 1902–1970**

'The Penguin Books are splendid value for sixpence, so splendid that if other publishers had any sense they would combine against them and suppress them'
**George Orwell**

'More than a business ... a national cultural asset'
**Guardian**

'When you look at the whole Penguin achievement you know that it constitutes, in action, one of the more democratic successes of our recent social history'
**Richard Hoggart**

# Young Bysshe

CLAIRE TOMALIN

PENGUIN BOOKS

PENGUIN BOOKS

Published by the Penguin Group
Penguin Books Ltd, 80 Strand, London WC2R ORL, England
Penguin Group (USA) Inc., 375 Hudson Street, New York, New York 10014, USA
Penguin Group (Canada), 10 Alcorn Avenue, Toronto, Ontario, Canada M4V 3B2
(a division of Pearson Penguin Canada Inc.)
Penguin Ireland, 25 St Stephen's Green, Dublin 2, Ireland
(a division of Penguin Books Ltd)
Penguin Group (Australia), 250 Camberwell Road, Camberwell, Victoria 3124,
Australia (a division of Pearson Australia Group Pty Ltd)
Penguin Books India Pvt Ltd, 11 Community Centre,
Panchsheel Park, New Delhi – 110 017, India
Penguin Group (NZ), cnr Airborne and Rosedale Roads, Albany,
Auckland 1310, New Zealand (a division of Pearson New Zealand Ltd)
Penguin Books (South Africa) (Pty) Ltd, 24 Sturdee Avenue,
Rosebank 2196, South Africa

Penguin Books Ltd, Registered Offices: 80 Strand, London WC2R ORL, England

www.penguin.com

*Shelley and his World* first published by Thames & Hudson 1980
First published in Penguin Books with revisions 1992
This extract published as a Pocket Penguin 2005

1

Set in 11.5/13.5pt Monotype Dante
Typeset by Palimpsest Book Production Limited
Polmont, Stirlingshire
Printed in England by Clays Ltd, St Ives plc

# Contents

## 1792–1811

Outside the village of Warnham in Sussex is a pond
as big as a small lake, surrounded by meadows set
with tall and splendid trees, a paradisal place for a
boy to spend a summer's day. The earliest letter of
Shelley's that we know – he was eleven when he
wrote it – was addressed to his cousin Kate, invit-
ing her and her brother Tom to spend a day, with
a picnic, at the pond, where his father kept a pleasure boat. To the end of his life, boats and water,
trees and grass were his symbols of blessedness,
Arcadia and Elysium in one. They dwelt in his
imagination, in his poetry, in the drawings scattered about his notebooks. Yet Shelley was not a
pastoral writer. What interested him was the power
of free thought and the spirit of revolution; and
these led him to break away from the privileged
security that seemed to be his birthright.

Percy Bysshe Shelley was born in 1792, a year
of portents. The English could hardly take their
eyes from France, where the momentum of revolution had carried the king to prison and stripped
the aristocracy and the Church of their power and

possessions; even domestic tyranny was under attack, with the first divorce laws passed. For some in England all this was inspiration. Tom Paine travelled the country, enthusiastically greeted by local revolutionary societies, and in London political clubs called for parliamentary reform and universal male suffrage. Paine published the second part of his *Rights of Man*, and an ex-governess, Mary Wollstonecraft, published her *A Vindication of the Rights of Woman*, both books that were to influence Shelley profoundly. A third was on the point of completion: William Godwin's masterwork, *Inquiry Concerning Political Justice*. In Germany a young Englishman, James Lawrence, was working on a book proposing the abolition of marriage, and total sexual and economic emancipation of women; this too would make its mark on Shelley. And a trio who were to give him his belief in the power of poetry to enter and change men's minds were just reaching maturity: Wordsworth at twenty-two visiting France, full of revolutionary enthusiasm; Coleridge and Southey, both university radicals.

But, for the majority of the English, any initial sympathy with the French Revolution was draining away in 1792 as reports of disorder and bloodshed grew worse. William Cowper withdrew his cautious approval, and Blake, who had been seen wearing a scarlet Jacobin cap, is said to have put it off. 'O! that

France had possessed the wisdom of knowing where to stop!' lamented the poet Anna Seward to her colleague Helen Maria Williams, resident in Paris. The novelist Fanny Burney, always nervous of the Revolution, took comfort from a talk with Edmund Burke over a Hampstead dinner table; he told her that even Charles James Fox had 'too much taste for such a Revolution'. When Burke was ribbed gently by his brother for his reactionary views, he turned to Miss Burney, filled her wineglass and drank a toast, 'Come, then – here's *Slavery forever!*' This was the year in which Burke split the Whig party, taking the majority over to support the Tories who wanted war with France. And war came in February 1793, bringing great misery to England, draining its finances and speeding inflation. The poor, both in the country and in the new industrial towns of the north, were brought to near-starvation. War meant too a vast buildup of armed forces, so that England began to look like an occupied country, with barracks everywhere and a discontented militia set over a powerless and embittered people. Finally, it meant that the upper and educated classes, accustomed to travel in Europe and enjoy its arts and ideas, were to be virtually confined to their own small island for two decades; it was at the end of this period that the word 'insular' began to be used in the sense of narrow-minded and prejudiced.

At Field Place in Sussex the world had already shrunk. True, the forty-year-old squire, Timothy Shelley, had been in parliament as a Whig protégé of the reforming Duke of Norfolk; but he was now unseated and had also recently found himself a wife, Elizabeth Pilfold, a handsome and well-bred young woman of twenty-nine. On 4 August their first child was born, in a room that looked out over the green garden to the fields and woods beyond. He was a blue-eyed boy and he was christened Percy Bysshe, and known thereafter in the family by his second name.

The Shelleys were an established Sussex family, but this particular branch had come into its prosperity only recently. Bysshe's grandfather, also Bysshe, was born in very modest circumstances in New Jersey, in America, and had to come to England to acquire a large fortune, chiefly by means of eloping with two successive heiresses. Old Bysshe educated his eldest son Timothy by sending him to Oxford and on the Grand Tour. He also built an enormous mansion, Castle Goring, for his family; but nobody wanted to live in it. Even he preferred to spend days in a cottage and evenings at the inn, when he was not visiting his mistress Mrs Nicholls and their four children – one actually called Bysshe – in Lambeth. Eccentric in some respects, he was a traditionalist in others: he was set on leaving a large, secure capital of money and estates for his legitimate male descendants, sharing fully in the belief of his day that the supreme value of the family resided in the prosperity of the male heirs. The granting of a baronetcy in 1806 put society's official seal of approval on the Shelleys.

Born into this agreeable inheritance, young Percy Bysshe was followed by five little sisters, one dying in infancy. For his first decade he lived at home, dominating this small female court; the pleasures of the situation may account for his lifelong propensity for setting up households of women around himself. His third sister Hellen remembered him as always good-tempered, full of pranks and vividly imaginative. He and his closest sister, Elizabeth, were supposed to resemble one another as though they had been twins, and from very early days they wrote verses together. He had a pony to gallop on and was taught field sports; shooting he loved all his life, although he came to prefer inanimate targets. At six he went daily to the local clergyman's house for Latin lessons. His memory was remarkable and his sisters remembered him reciting Latin verses to their father, who was proud of his accomplished son. It was a kind, conventional family. And when Bysshe was ten he was sent, conventionally, away to school.

The Syon House Academy at Brentford was run

by a gruff Dr Greenlaw and his wife; there were about sixty boys rising to the age of eighteen and as rough as any such group of boys is likely to be. Shelley's older cousin Tom Medwin, who was already there, says the place was 'a perfect hell' to the slight, girlish-looking child. He took refuge in solitary musing and the reading of Gothic romances, the cheapest and most plentiful popular entertainment in print then; they sated his appetite for reading and excited his imagination with ghosts and terrors.

The school did offer Shelley one thing that caught his interest. A travelling lecturer, Dr Adam Walker, friend of the great radical scientist Joseph Priestley, came to speak to the boys about chemistry and the scientific advances of the day. Impressed by the talk of electricity, telescopes and magnetism, Shelley carried home his enthusiasm to share with his admiring and sometimes frightened sisters. There was a plan to cure their chilblains by passing electric currents through them; on another occasion, putting science to the service of fiction, he persuaded them to dress up as fiends and accompany him as he pranced through the house with a bowl of burning spirits in his hand; and he mysteriously hinted of an alchemist living concealed in a certain room in the attic.

His two years' initiation into the rougher world of boys was a preparation for Eton. There he remained for six years, the longest stable residence of his life, from 1804 to 1810. (While he was there the youngest Shelley child, John, was born in 1806.) Dr Keate, known as 'Flogger', became Provost during Shelley's time, but the masters were less troublesome to him than the boys, who at once perceived that they had someone odd to bait and took great pleasure in driving gentle Shelley into a mad, white, shaking and raging creature. In later years his friend Thomas Love Peacock and his wife Mary were to hear of his intense sufferings and also of how he once stabbed another boy with a fork in his anger.

There was much for Shelley to find objectionable at Eton:

> . . . there rose
> From the near schoolroom, voices, that, alas!
> Were but one echo from a world of woes –
> The harsh and grating strife of tyrants and of foes.

– is how he put it later in *The Revolt of Islam*; and 'nothing that my tyrants knew or taught / I cared to learn'. He detested the fagging system, whereby younger boys bought protection from older ones by performing menial services for them: '*obedience*

7

is a word which in my opinion should have no existence', he told his father later. Studies were virtually confined to the reading of Latin and Greek and making of verses in those languages, child's play to Shelley but not calculated to hold his attention: he was much more interested in chemistry. Lacking instruction, he was drawn by the quasi-magical power of science, and had not the temperament for slow, patiently repeated experiment and observation. In visionary fashion, he imagined a world transformed by electricity, Africa explored by balloon, infertile soil made productive. Pursuing such prophetic notions, he forgot to tie his shoelaces or wear a hat; to his conventional peers such opinions and behaviour earned him the title of 'mad Shelley'.

The intellectual guidance and companionship he failed to find at Eton were provided in his last two years there by the elderly Dr James Lind, one of George III's physicians, who lived in Windsor and took a fancy to the clever, enthusiastic boy. Lind, Edinburgh-born and connected with the radical, scientific Lunar Society that flourished in the 1780s and brought together men such as Joseph Priestley, Erasmus Darwin and James Watt, had also travelled as far afield as India and China. He was a prime instance of British Enlightenment man and he played a crucial part in Shelley's development.

Under Lind's influence Shelley began to learn modern languages – French and German – and to read seriously. He absorbed the works of Lucretius (*De rerum natura*), whose anti-religious views pleased him, Pliny (*Historia naturalis*), Franklin and Condorcet, another deeply anti-religious writer whose views on human progress and perfectibility made a permanent mark on his thinking. He also discovered the English philosopher who was to shape the course of his life dramatically: William Godwin. No doubt Shelley was drawn first to Godwin's novel *St Leon*, whose hero possesses the Elixir Vitae and the Philosopher's Stone. But he went on to read *Political Justice* and make its serenely reasonable and optimistic principles his own. *Political Justice* is in essence an attack on government – which Godwin described as intending to suppress injustice but actually embodying and perpetuating it – and indeed on all institutions which ossify behaviour and thinking. By free inquiry, Godwin believed that mankind would necessarily arrive at a state of contented anarchy; crime and even insincerity would slowly disappear, and the equal distribution of wealth would be accepted by all as an essential basis for human happiness. To Shelley, as to the young Wordsworth, these ideas came with the force of revelation.

Eton undoubtedly caused him to suffer, and he

was at times inclined to describe it as a microcosm of the evils of the world at large. But his memories were not all black. He made some friends with whom he enjoyed exploring the gentle Berkshire fields and woods along the banks of the Thames, and the lines he wrote in 1821 in *The Boat on the Serchio* suggest good moments:

> 'Those bottles of warm tea –
> (Give me some straw) – must be stowed tenderly;
> Such as we used, in summer after six,
> To cram in greatcoat pockets, and to mix
> Hard eggs and radishes and rolls at Eton,
> And, couched on stolen hay in those green harbours
> Farmers called gaps, and we schoolboys called arbours,
> Would feast till eight.'

In his last school year he published a novel, *Zastrozzi*, giving a banquet for eight of his friends with part of the proceeds; this is not the action of a wholly isolated and martyred boy.

*Zastrozzi* is a Gothic tale of vengeance and passion, closely modelled on the trash Shelley had comforted himself with at Syon Academy. The plot turns on the pursuit of a dazed hero by a wicked beauty determined to seduce him, and concludes with general bloodshed. Shelley put his initials on the title-page, and an epigraph taken from *Paradise*

*Lost*, the earliest token of his lifelong admiration for Milton, whose career as both political pamphleteer and poet he would emulate.

He was already writing poetry. Just after leaving school, and due to go to Oxford in October 1810, he published his first volume, *Original Poetry by Victor and Cazire*. It contained some rattling verse epistles by sister Elizabeth and sentimental lyrics, Gothic ballads and alleged translations from the German and Italian by Bysshe. If booby prizes were given for the juvenilia of great poets, *Victor and Cazire* would carry one off. To crown matters, it included an entire poem lifted from the Gothic author known as 'Monk' Lewis; when the publisher asked Shelley about this he offered no explanation, but insisted on the destruction of all unsold copies. Nearly 1,500 had been printed; the episode leaves a small question-mark over his reliability and judgement, boy as he was.

A copy of *Victor and Cazire* was sent by Shelley to his cousin Harriet Grove in Wiltshire. It was not an idle gift. Harriet's mother and Mrs Shelley were sisters, the families very close and a mutual attraction between the cousins smiled upon. The girl, a year older than Bysshe, was pretty and affectionate; her diary could have been penned by one of Jane Austen's young ladies. She records a great many walks, games of battledore, bathing in the sea and dances. She reads a little: Sterne's *Sentimental Journey* and an anti-Godwinite novel, *The Modern Philosophers*. It made her laugh, but would have outraged Shelley, who fell in love with her and wished to convert her to his views.

Her devotion to her Etonian cousin, 'dear Bysshe' and then 'dearest Percy', is evident. The high point is reached when both families stay in London in the spring of 1810 and the young pair are allowed a good deal of licence, walking in Lincoln's Inn Fields and disliking the opera together. But by the end of the year she has nothing more to say of him, and by January 1811 Shelley is agonizedly attributing their severance to her disapproval of his anti-religious views. Possibly this was so; there is no sign of family pressure in her diary and attempts to eradicate references to him suggest that she suffered her own change of heart. She married a neighbouring landowner's son and lived the sort of uneventful life poets wish on their daughters more often than their mistresses. For Shelley, the year 1811 was to see him carried irrevocably out of the world of custom and ceremony.

Oxford in 1810 was more of a finishing school for well-to-do young men than a place of learning, run by college Fellows who were obliged to take holy orders. According to Jeremy Bentham most were morose, insipid or profligate. The

Bodleian, one of the finest libraries in Europe, went almost unused. University College, where Shelley was to go, differed in no way from the rest; even the young niece of the Master, paying a visit from Scotland, delivered the tart verdict that 'the very meaning of the word education did not seem to be understood'.

Still, Shelley arrived with every prospect of being comfortable. He was attending his father's college; Timothy, proudly escorting him, had his rooms newly furnished. He also took his son to see the Oxford booksellers and printers, Slatter & Munday, to whom he made the most famous remark of his life: 'My son here has a literary turn; he is already an author, and do pray indulge him in his printing freaks.'

A few days later another important meeting took place when, over dinner in hall, Shelley came face to face with Thomas Jefferson Hogg, son of a Yorkshire barrister and a vigorous and original young man. An immediate and passionate friendship sprang up between the two. Hogg's portrait of Shelley, written from the vantage point of somewhat cynical middle age, still breathes a strong, sardonic affection, and the Oxford chapters are particularly engaging.

Through his eyes we see Shelley, tall, slight and stooped, going about Oxford with his characteristic hasty step, coatless and open-necked; hear his high, cracked voice; see him reading with the book always held right up to his eyes, or lying so close to the fire that he seemed more salamander than mortal. Now he is running headlong into his sported oak – the outer door to college rooms – and now tramping through the Oxfordshire mud with his pistols, enraged when a farm dog tears the skirts of his new, blue, brass-buttoned tailcoat, delighted with a paper boat or a conversation with a gypsy child. His view of the dons was lordly:

'They are very dull people here,' Shelley said to me one evening . . . 'a little man sent for me this morning, and told me in an almost inaudible whisper that I must read: "you must read", he said many times in his small voice . . . I told him I had some books in my pocket, and began to take them out. He stared at me, and said that was not exactly what he meant: "you must read *Prometheus Vinctus*, and Demosthenes *de Coronâ*, and Euclid." "Must I read Euclid?" I asked sorrowfully . . .'

Hogg's description of Shelley's rooms transforms them into a sorcerer's cave:

Books, boots, papers, shoes, philosophical instruments, clothes, pistols, linen, crockery, ammunition, and phials innumerable, with money, stockings, prints, crucibles, bags, and boxes were scattered on the floor and in every place . . . The tables, and especially the carpet, were already stained with large spots of various hues, which frequently proclaimed the agency of fire. An electrical machine, an air pump, the galvanic trough, a solar microscope, and large glass jars and receivers, were conspicuous amidst the mass of matter.

By the end of his first term Shelley had decided that Hogg must bind their friendship still closer by wooing his sister Elizabeth. Letters from Field Place elaborated on this plan alongside laments over the 'uncongenial jollities of Xmas', the loss of Harriet and some fierce disputes with his father over the question of religious faith. Mrs Shelley became alarmed by her son's tendencies too: 'My mother fancies me on the High Road to Pandemonium, she fancies I want to make a deistical coterie of all my little sisters.' And it was true that Shelley was now able to assail conventional Christian belief with every logical weapon from the Enlightenment armoury; he was encouraged by Hogg, who sent him 'a systematic cudgel for Xtianity' during the vacation.

His father's hope was that he would enter for a poetry prize when he returned for the Lent term. He had published a second novel, *St Irvyne, or the Rosicrucian*, 'by a Gentleman of the University of

Oxford', written to much the same formula as *Zastrozzi* but with additional supernatural elements. Although it was now on display in Slatter & Munday's window it deserved to be, and was, a failure. Another publication was a volume of poems, *Posthumous Fragments of Margaret Nicholson* by 'John Fitzvictor'. The humour of the title was that Mrs Nicholson was a mad washerwoman who had attempted to kill George III in 1786; it was not much of a joke, and the poems are inept whether political, erotic or lamenting lost happiness. But here and there a glimpse of later themes appears. An invocation to despair contains a Shelleyan turn of phrase:

> Arise ye sightless spirits of the storm.
> Ye unseen minstrels of the aëreal song . . .

and another poem produces a characteristic encounter. 'I met a maniac, like he was to me.' This was not a merely poetic notion; Shelley told Hogg and other friends that 'I myself am often mad.' His cousin Medwin believed that 'insanity hung as by a hair suspended over the head of Shelley' and there were times when not only his family but also, later, so close and sympathetic an observer as Thomas Love Peacock took the view that his behaviour passed beyond the bounds of the normal.

In March Shelley wrote to his father saying he was getting on with his prize poem on the Parthenon. He was also quietly busy with the other interests. He subscribed a guinea to a fund for an Irish journalist, Peter Finnerty, sentenced to prison for political outspokenness, and offered to write a poem in his defence; and wrote to Leigh Hunt, editor of the liberal magazine, the *Examiner*, who had tangled with the powers of the land more than once. To Hunt, Shelley suggested that he intended to follow his father into parliament.

Meanwhile, he had printed a very short pamphlet incorporating Hogg's and his own arguments against Christianity, claiming the necessity for free inquiry into religious belief and suggesting that the existence of God remained unproven by physical evidence, reason or testimony. He had it printed in Worthing, by the same firm that published his unfortunate *Original Poetry*, and sent to him at Oxford. It was called *The Necessity of Atheism*, the title markedly more pugnacious than the contents; and when the copies arrived he sent some off to various bishops and heads of colleges. He also went into Slatter & Munday's shop and laid some out on the counters, where they remained for twenty minutes until they caught the eye of a passing Fellow of New College, who went into the shop and easily persuaded the astonished proprietors to burn them all at once. Shelley now sent a copy to the Professor of Poetry, accompanied by a letter signed 'Jeremiah Stukely'. The Professor showed this to the Master of University College, who in turn summoned Shelley on the morning of 25 March. In the presence of a few irritated Fellows, first Shelley and then Hogg refused to answer questions as to the authorship of the pamphlet and both were summarily expelled from the University. According to Hogg, Shelley was in a state of acute excitement and distress.

## 1811–1814

The two young men arrived in London the next day, found themselves a room in a coffee-house and called at once on Harriet Grove's brothers in Lincoln's Inn Fields where, according to Hogg, they were rather quietly received at first. Shelley was desperate to talk. At four in the morning he roused another cousin, Tom Medwin, knocking and laughing and calling out, 'I am expelled – for atheism.' The next morning he and Hogg set out to find proper lodgings, alighting in rooms off Oxford Street which caught Shelley's fancy because they were papered in a pattern of green and purple grapes on a trellis. Here they settled, planning to resume their reading and walking habits and to stay together. The Grove cousins proved friendly; John was a surgeon, Charles a medical student, and Shelley attended a course of lectures on anatomy at St Bartholomew's Hospital with a fleeting thought of taking up medicine himself. He also went with them to a debating club, where he attracted attention as a speaker but fled without giving his name.

Two of his sisters, Hellen and Mary, were at boarding school on Clapham Common, where Shelley had already met their friend Harriet Westbrook, who was quite prepared to join them in sympathetic hero-worship of Bysshe. Harriet was fifteen, the prettiest girl in the school, with brilliant pink cheeks, a vast quantity of curls and a perfect readiness to listen to Shelley's opinions and adopt them as her own. Not surprisingly, he found some comfort in his visits to Clapham.

Timothy Shelley's reaction to the news of his son's expulsion was to come to London, attempt to separate him from Hogg, whom he at first blamed, and insist that Shelley should return home and take instruction from a clergyman. When the two met, the father cursed, wept and insisted on reading out Archdeacon Paley's arguments for the existence of God. The son laughed derisively, the more so because his father mispronounced Paley as 'Pally'. Both were slightly hysterical. A little later, Mrs Shelley privately sent her son money for his journey home; but he returned it.

Money now became of prime importance in the struggle, and Timothy Shelley continued to use it as his weapon until his death. Old Sir Bysshe supported Timothy against young Bysshe, and it was decided that he must cool his heels and deal only through the family lawyer, William Whitton.

Shelley stood to inherit over £200,000 in due course; he showed his disregard for the values of his family by suggesting to Whitton that the entail, which covered £80,000 of the estate, should be set aside and that part divided between Mrs Shelley and the girls. He would be content, meanwhile, with an annuity of £100 or £200. Timothy was almost as much shocked by this piece of disrespect for property as by his son's atheism. And although Shelley came to hate the poverty in which he lived most of his life, and was sometimes culpably careless about debts, he was never acquisitive and never wanted anything more than a competence for himself.

In mid-April Hogg, won over and forgiven by his family, departed for a holiday before going home to York to take up legal studies. Deprived of his friend, Shelley was naturally lonely. He kept a journal in which he described his dreams, and began to sleepwalk as he had done in times of stress at school and would again when life was difficult. Sometimes Medwin went to Kensington Gardens with him and watched him sail boats on the Serpentine; there were still the Grove brothers; and now the Westbrooks – for Harriet had a much older sister, Eliza – began to fill up the emptiness. Harriet is reported as reading Voltaire in May, and being persecuted at school for the atheism she has learnt from Shelley. Her father, a well-to-do coffee-house proprietor, no doubt saw the advantage of his daughter's friendship with the rich, susceptible heir to a baronetcy and fortune, and Shelley was made welcome at the Westbrook house. By the time he left London for Sussex in May, he had arranged that Harriet and he should correspond; but her letters were to go to his uncle Pilfold's house at Cuckfield, not to Field Place.

Shelley went to Cuckfield because this maternal uncle was friendly and prepared to help the warring father and son to an agreement of sorts. Bysshe was to have £200 a year and live where he chose; he also agreed to take up a profession. His mother, he told Hogg, with whom he corresponded unceasingly, was 'quite rational'. 'She says . . . if a man is a good man, atheist or Xtian he will do very well in whatever future state awaits us. This I call liberality.' But his sister Elizabeth was decidedly cool, especially when he attempted to press Hogg's love on her – a love dreamt up out of the air by Shelley, for the two had not met. Shelley's letters were full of attacks on the institution of marriage, and his hope was that Hogg and his sister would form a free-love union. A clandestine visit by Hogg in which he was smuggled into Field Place and kept concealed in Shelley's room did nothing to further the suit.

Shelley was cheered through the confusions of these months by a new friend, Elizabeth Hitchener, a Sussex schoolmistress who taught one of his Pilfold cousins. Miss Hitchener was ten years older than Shelley and the daughter of an innkeeper; she was unusual in her abilities and independence of mind (and also in physical appearance, for she was strikingly tall and dark). She inclined to feminism and republicanism: opinions of this kind had to be kept to oneself in Sussex in 1811. The friendship and correspondence with Shelley must have been a huge relief from intellectual isolation. He in turn wrote to her that, although he was cautious in his theological speculations,

in politics – here I am enthusiastic. I have reasoned, and my reason has brought me on this subject to the end of my inquiries. I am no aristocrat, nor 'crat' at all, but vehemently long for the time when men may dare to live in accordance with Nature and Reason – in consequence, with Virtue, to which I firmly believe that Religion and its establishments, Polity and its establishments, are the formidable though destructible barriers.

And he complained, very reasonably, of the folly of the Prince Regent's ball at Carlton House in June, for which £120,000 was spent on splendours that included an artificial stream in which goldfish swam between moss banks – all this when bad harvests and inflation had brought the people to terrible distress, the Lancashire mill workers were on a three-day week and machines were being smashed. Shelley began an English version of the *Marseillaise* with the lines

> Tremble, Kings despised of man!
> Ye traitors to your Country . . .

Poor George III, grief-struck at the death of his youngest daughter, had, in fact, lapsed into madness again. All through 1811 signs of his recovery were looked for in vain while his son prepared to take over the position of ruling monarch by abandoning any liberal principles he had once boasted.

Shelley's political views had now taken permanent shape. He had absorbed the lessons of Condorcet, Thomas Paine and Godwin, all of whom believed in the power of the human mind to change the circumstances of life for the better unless prevented by established institutions such as the monarchy and the Church; but all of whom equally developed reservations about overthrowing them by violence. He had also observed for himself the gulf between rich and poor, usually

justified to young people of his class by reference
to the will of God. To Shelley, this explanation
was unacceptable. For the rest of his life he
remained true to his detestation of monarchy,
aristocracy, huge fortunes, the established Church
and standing armies. He remained a reformer,
always hoping to see reform brought about by
reasonable means and despairing when blood was
shed even by insurgents with a just cause; and he
retained his belief in the necessity of redistribut-
ing wealth.

He also retained his dislike of the institution of
marriage as a tie unnecessary between those who
care for one another and terrible between those
who do not. In spite of this he was persuaded to
marry in 1811, partly because he saw the force of
the argument that free love, in the social and
medical circumstances of the day, was likely to put
women into more difficulties than men. He was
also captivated by Harriet Westbrook's beauty,
distress and trust in him; and perhaps made more
vulnerable by the estrangement from a family of
sisters and girl cousins who had been supremely
important to him all through his early years.
Defiance of his father was another good reason for
marrying: Timothy Shelley (according to Medwin)
told him that he would provide for any number of
bastards but would not forgive a *mésalliance*. Such

a remark from an uncongenial father to an ideal-
istic boy of eighteen is calculated to put him on
the path of knight errantry; and Shelley, like his
friend Leigh Hunt, was shocked by the sexual
callousness of a society which used armies of pros-
titutes while professing to observe Christian ideals
of marriage.

After spending a week in London in early July,
and seeing the Westbrooks again, Shelley paid a visit
to his cousin Thomas Grove's estate, Cwm Elan, in
Wales. From there he wrote to both Hogg and Miss
Hitchener to say that Harriet was in love with him,
had told him so, was suffering persecution at school
and had thrown herself on his protection. She meanwhile sent him a copy of a book by Amelia Opie,
one-time friend of William Godwin and his wife
Mary Wollstonecraft; the point of Mrs Opie's novel,
*Adeline Mowbray*, was to show the evils arising from
even a principled decision not to marry, the hero-
ine's position becoming really desperate when she
finds herself pregnant. Possibly Shelley knew by
now that his hero Godwin had himself succumbed
to a marriage ceremony with Mary Wollstonecraft
in just those circumstances.

At all events, on 25 August Shelley and Harriet
– who were now just nineteen and sixteen respec-
tively – met in London, spent the day hiding in a
coffee-house, and took the night coach for Scotland

where they were married, after three days of almost non-stop travel. He had less than £50 of borrowed money in his pockets. Within a few days of the wedding he persuaded Hogg to join him and Harriet in Edinburgh, setting up the pattern of a *ménage* of at least three which he found essential to happiness. Hogg was enchanted by Harriet, and the three of them spent their time reading and translating – Shelley began on the French naturalist and historian Buffon, Harriet on a French romance – and visiting the Edinburgh kirks to laugh at the sermons. In the evenings Harriet read aloud while, according to Hogg, her husband fell asleep on the hearth-rug.

The chief problem was money. As soon as Timothy heard of his son's marriage he stopped his allowance. Shelley wrote angry complaints to his father and his grandfather:

The institutions of society have made you, tho' liable to be misled by passion and prejudice like others, the *Head of the family* . . .

– a situation Shelley himself could not be imagined in; and later,

Think not I am an insect whom injuries destroy – had I money enough I would meet you in London, & hollow

27

in your ears Bysshe, Bysshe, Bysshe, – aye Bysshe till you're deaf.

He went so far as to accuse his father of wishing him dead, developing a fantasy that he would have liked him conscripted for the Peninsular War and killed in Spain. He also made a wild accusation of adultery against his mother, fortunately not seen by the family, since by then all letters were passed unopened to Whitton.

Early in October the three runaways left Edinburgh for York, so that Hogg could continue his studies. Shelley now informed Miss Hitchener, after several weeks' silence, that he was married, and her warm response led him to hail her as sister of his soul; in addition, he proposed that she should come and live as part of his household. Eliza Westbrook was also summoned. Meanwhile, he set off for Sussex again, leaving Harriet and Hogg in York. His trip was a vain one; he got no money and was further estranged from his mother and sisters; Whitton referred to him as 'a mad viper'. He returned to York in low spirits to find a crisis there too. In his absence, Harriet told him, Hogg had attempted to seduce her; and she and Eliza Westbrook insisted on leaving York at once, without informing Hogg. Shelley was in agony; his love for Hogg was as great as his love for Harriet and, as he wrote to Elizabeth

Hitchener, 'his vices and not himself' were the objects of my horror'. Impassioned letters of mingled reproach, forgiveness and desolation at losing his friend flew from Keswick, where the Shelley party had fled, to York. He attempted to explain that it was not his prejudice that stood between the friends:

Jealousy has no place in my bosom, I am indeed at times very much inclined to think that the Godwinian plan is best . . . But Harriet does not think so. She is prejudiced: tho' I hope she will not always be so – And on her opinions of right and wrong alone does the morality of the present case depend.

Possibly he would have shared Harriet gladly with Hogg had she been willing; but she was not, and his spirits were in turmoil, whether from simple disappointment at Hogg's baseness or a more complicated response to the effect of marriage on friendship.

By the end of November he was calmer. He and Harriet and Eliza were settled at Chestnut Cottage, one of a group a mile outside Keswick. He began to notice the scenery and describe it:

These gigantic mountains piled on each other, these waterfalls, these million-shaped clouds tinted by the

varying colours of innumerable rainbows hanging
between yourself and the lake as smooth and dark as
a plain of polished jet . . .

On 1 December the party went to stay at
Greystoke, the house of the Duke of Norfolk, who
was trying to reconcile the father and son. Shelley
did agree to write a letter of apology, though insist-
ing that he would not conceal his political or religious opinions, and Timothy relented: the allowance
was restored.

One of his hopes in going to the Lakes was to
meet Southey, whose poetry he had admired from
childhood but whose 'tergiversation' on political
matters he intended to reproach him with: 'he to
whom Bigotry, Tyranny, Law was hateful, has
become the votary of those idols in a form most
disgusting'. Shelley despised Southey for his
support of the war in Spain, of the Church of
England and of the rotten English constitution; and
contrasted him with Wordsworth, who lived in
poverty and integrity (and proved inaccessible).
When Southey and Shelley actually met they took
to one another in spite of their disagreements.
Southey, at thirty-eight, convinced himself that
Shelley's errors were all attributable to youth, and
complacently told him that he would change as
Southey himself had done. 'He will get rid of his

eccentricity, and he will retain his morals, his integrity and his genius,' he wrote confidently to a friend. Shelley was less certain; he admired Southey for supporting a large household of dependants, but thought him 'corrupted by the world, contaminated by Custom'.

A precious testimony of Shelley at this time was given in 1890 by a very old lady who remembered him calling on her family when she was eight:

I think I remember best the sort of look that came upon my father's and upon Southey's face when he talked, and how I and my brother were turned out of the room.

The spoken word is often thought to be dangerous to children; and of course Shelley was interested in them, and wanted to win their minds. In January 1812 he wrote to his sister Hellen, the last member of his family of whom he had hopes, asked her about her reading and said: '*Thinking*, and thinking without letting anything but *reason* influence your mind, is the great thing.' But she never saw the letter, which was intercepted and sent to Whitton.

The general response to proclaimed atheism at this time can be judged by one of the *Tales* (1812) of a popular enough poet, Crabbe. His story tells of a country boy who reads the 'modern philosophy' in

London and has to be cured of his atheism by his father, whose method is simple – he whips the 'learned boy' until he is nearly skinned. Crabbe was not regarded as an inhumane man; what lay behind such attitudes was the real dread inspired by the French Revolution, a dread which drove the English into a smug rejection of intellectual inquiry because it had proved dangerous to life and property. The older Romantic poets, Southey and Coleridge and Wordsworth, in one way and another came to minister to this smugness; it became Shelley's serious endeavour, on the other hand, to persuade people if possible that free inquiry remained good in itself and did not necessarily lead to violence.

Shelley learnt from Southey one fact that filled him with 'inconceivable emotion': that William Godwin was not, like Buffon and Voltaire and Hume, among the honourable dead, but alive and resident in London. One of his first acts in 1812 was to write to him, declare himself his disciple and beg for a meeting. Godwin's cautious response evoked a long autobiographical letter from Shelley; and the friendship, destined to become one of the oddest in English literary history, was established.

In his third letter to Godwin, Shelley announced his intention of going to Ireland to promote the cause of Catholic Emancipation: under English government the majority of the Irish people had few political or property rights, and very limited access to education or professions. Shelley's interest in the cause may well have been encouraged by the Duke of Norfolk, who was much concerned with it; but Godwin wrote nervously, suggesting that his disciple should return instead to London, fearing he was 'preparing a scene of blood'. In fact his intentions were entirely pacific.

He did not set off for Dublin at once. During January he suffered from 'nervous attacks', for which he dosed himself with laudanum, an opium-based drug taken as readily then as aspirin or tranquillizers today. Possibly the drug worked on Shelley's imagination; at all events he either imagined he was or was actually attacked at the cottage door one Sunday evening. A neighbour, hearing noise, came running and found him lying senseless. Harriet was at first very frightened; Shelley himself later made light of the incident. He continued the use of laudanum throughout his life.

This particular trouble was forgotten in the bustle of preparing to leave for Dublin; he hoped to observe conditions there, make contact with politicians and write and distribute pamphlets. The first of these, an *Address to the Irish People*, couched in the simplest language, urged them to patience, sobriety, hard work, religious tolerance and the avoidance of violence; and painted an idyllic picture of the good society that might evolve from such conduct, with political freedom and economic equality ensuring perfect happiness. The pamphlet was advertised, sent to leading figures, posted up in taverns and handed out in the street with Harriet's assistance.

A second pamphlet, aimed at the educated public, *Proposals for an Association*, suggested setting up an organization to work for the repeal of the 1800 Act of Union (with England) as well as for Catholic rights. Shelley spoke on this theme one evening at a public meeting in the Fishamble Street Theatre, packed with well-dressed people, for Daniel O'Connell was the first speaker. Shelley's delivery was very slow, with pauses between the sentences which allowed the audience to applaud when he attacked English oppression and hiss when he deplored religious bigotry.

His seven weeks in Dublin gave him no great opinion of its political leaders, and they had no time for him; but he was horribly impressed by the poverty which swarmed even in Sackville Street, outside his lodgings. A young widow with three infants was arrested for stealing a penny loaf before his eyes; he interceded for her but acknowledged that she was far gone in drunkenness. He was not sentimental about the brutalized Irish poor:

Intemperance and hard labour have reduced them to machines. The oyster that is washed and driven at the mercy of the tides appears to me an animal of almost equal elevation in the scale of intellectual being.

He did not think society ready for universal suffrage, but he composed an exalted *Declaration of Rights* on the American and French patterns, and had it printed in Ireland. The conflict between his wish for radical change and his dislike of coercion emerges clearly:

The rights of man are liberty, and an equal participation of the commonage of nature . . .

The rights of man in the present state of society, are only to be secured by some degree of coercion to be exercised on their violator.

The sufferer has a right that the degree of coercion employed be as slight as possible . . .

No man has the right to disturb the public peace, by personally resisting the execution of a law however bad. He ought to acquiesce, using at the same time the utmost powers of his reason, to promote its repeal . . .

No man has a right to do an evil thing that good may come . . .

Expediency is inadmissible in morals. Politics are only sound when conducted on principles of morality . . .

At the same time he turned out a satirical poem, *The Devil's Walk*, whose chief merit lies in its fore-shadowing of a much later one, *The Masque of Anarchy*, in certain lines:

> The hell-hounds, Murder, Want and Woe,
>     Forever hungering, flocked around;
> From Spain had Satan sought their food,
>     'Twas human woe and human blood!

Shelley was not yet a poet in achievement or even primarily in intention; he was far more interested in writing essays on political and moral themes, and he was some way through a novel about pre-revolutionary France, 'Hubert Cauvin'. (It never appeared; and the manuscript is lost.)

Before leaving Ireland in April 1812, Shelley posted off a box of his *Declaration of Rights* pamphlets to Miss Hitchener. Then he, Harriet, Eliza and an Irish servant called Dan Healy (or Hill) embarked for Wales, hoping to settle on a farm near his cousin Thomas Grove. This plan fell through for lack of money, and they moved south to Lynmouth, on the north coast of Devon, at the end of June. Here Miss Hitchener was to join them, after some hesitation and many attempts to dissuade her by her parents and the Pilfolds, all suspicious of the nature of the love Shelley was offering – had he not written to her that he regarded marriage as 'an evil of immense and extensive magnitude . . . monopolizing, exclusive, jealous'? His opinions on this subject were strongly influenced by his reading of Lawrence's *Empire of the Nairs, or the Rights of Women, an Utopian Romance*. Lawrence, another Old Etonian, had written his book in Germany in 1793, where it was greeted as an extension of Mary Wollstonecraft's work and taken entirely seriously; but it was not translated into English until 1811. Shelley had a copy and wrote of it: 'Perfectly and decidedly do I subscribe to the truth of the principles which it is designed to establish.' The principles are that sexual constancy, even to an excellent spouse, is impossible; that the present system makes marriage a profession for ladies and prostitution the trade of less fortunate women; and that the abolition of marriage, with inheritance through the female line and children brought up by their mothers, financially supported by the state if necessary, would be a far better system. 'Let every female live perfectly uncontrolled by any man, and enjoying every freedom . . . let her choose and change her love as she please,' suggested Lawrence.

Shelley's enthusiastic endorsement of Lawrence was not a passing fad; in 1814 he gave the book to his two women companions to study. Whether either Harriet or Miss Hitchener read it is not recorded. At all events his enthusiasm for Miss Hitchener was entirely intellectual and Harriet, ever ready to join him in his feelings, was as eager for her arrival as he was.

Their keenness to extend their household was so great that Shelley wondered if Godwin might also be persuaded to join them; he declined, but planned a reconnaissance trip to Lynmouth for the late summer.

The remote village of Lynmouth, with its beach on to the Bristol Channel and steeply rising hills behind, delighted Shelley. The cottage was small, the landlady kind, and he began to amass a library. His two passions, for the acquisition of books and for travel, standing in direct opposition to one another, meant that 'a large share of his scanty income . . . was always expended upon books' and, as Hogg goes on to say, 'what an excellent collection of valuable books the poor poet would have owned if all his different libraries, scattered about in different localities, had been brought together under one roof'. The title of 'poet' was beginning to be appropriate. Shelley was at work on what he described modestly to his bookseller Thomas

Hookham as a 'little poem' to be called *Queen Mab*.

But *Queen Mab* was set aside in June in favour of another political pamphlet, the *Letter to Lord Ellenborough*. It is a defence of the bookseller Daniel Isaac Eaton, who had been sentenced by Lord Ellenborough to eighteen months' imprisonment and the pillory once a month, for publishing the third part of Tom Paine's *Age of Reason*. Eaton was a radical and indeed a republican; his trial was a travesty, with the judge constantly interrupting his defence. In his *Letter* Shelley pointed out that Eaton was really on trial for holding an opinion; that there was no necessary connection between religion and morality, and that while the economic security of the Church might be threatened by unbelievers, the word of God should not need the protection of the law. It is heartening to know that Eaton was cheered when brought out to the pillory, because it was intended as a way of delivering victims over to mob violence; people were pelted to death there in the eighteenth century.

Shelley had his pamphlet printed at the nearby town of Barnstaple and sent copies to Hookham with instructions to show them only to friends 'who are not informers'. He was right to be cautious, even if his caution was a patchy thing. The government had already been informed about the box containing his *Declaration of Rights* leaflets, which was opened by the Customs at Holyhead. And now he took to distributing them by a new method: he rowed out into the Bristol Channel and sent them forth in bottles or home-made boats. Others he launched more dramatically from the hilltop at dusk in a fire balloon. Both exercises inspired him to sonnets:

Bright ball of flame that through the gloom of even
 Silently takest thine aethereal way,
 And with surpassing glory dimm'st each ray
Twinkling amid the dark blue depths of Heaven . . .

Half-way through July his fellow radical, Miss Hitchener, finally arrived to cheer them and celebrate Harriet's seventeenth and Shelley's twentieth birthdays at the beginning of August.

Shelley's next move was to send his servant Dan to Barnstaple with copies of the *Declaration of Rights* and *The Devil's Walk*, telling him to post some on buildings and hand out others to passers-by. He had taken the precaution of cutting off the printer's name, and it was this offence that led to Dan's speedy arrest. With Irish ingenuity Dan insisted that his instructions had come from a strange gentleman in black; but he was sentenced to six months' imprisonment. Shelley appealed in vain for his release but was permitted to pay fifteen

shillings a week towards easing his prison conditions. Meanwhile, the town clerk wrote to the
Secretary of State, Lord Sidmouth, to inform him
of what had passed. The local postmaster had
already sent a copy of the *Declaration* to the
Secretary of the Post Office. But although Shelley
had impressed the inhabitants of Devon with his
activities, the Home Office advised that no action
should be taken against him. For the moment, in
any case, home affairs were overshadowed by news
from abroad: in August Wellington marched into
Madrid, and in September Napoleon made his fatal
entry into Moscow.

Shelley was unmolested, but penniless once
more and obliged to borrow from his landlady Mrs
Hooper, who was so taken with him that she went
out to borrow more funds from her neighbours
for his relief. With this, he and his three ladies left
Lynmouth at the end of August, forgetting about
Godwin's plan to call on them; when the philosopher arrived in September he had to find what
consolation he could in hearing Mrs Hooper sing
Shelley's praises. There is an envious comment by
Hogg on the instant favour his friend found with
the women in any household, from mistress to
maid; and it is true that nobody ever thought him
ordinary, partly, perhaps, because alongside the
manners of a well-bred young man there was none

of the usual arrogance of his class and sex. He was neither sanctimonious nor cynical, and inclined to take everyone he met seriously, an unusual experience for most women. Accounts of his physical appearance vary but agree that his hair was abundant and curly and usually in wild disorder; that his head was small, as were all his features except his eyes, which were a remarkable deep blue, 'large and animated, with a dash of wildness'; and his skin was fair and freckled. Leigh Hunt's description confirms the angelic air so many saw:

His side-face . . . was deficient in strength, and his features would not have told well in a bust; but when fronting and looking at you attentively his aspect had a certain seraphical character that would have suited a portrait of John the Baptist or the angel whom Milton describes as holding a reed 'tipt with fire'.

The party moved first to Ilfracombe and then into Wales again, where they travelled north until they reached a village exactly calculated to appeal to his interest in man's ability to reconstruct the world on a better plan than God's. William Madocks, MP, had reclaimed an area of land from the sea marshes already, built the model village of Tremadoc and established farms; he was now constructing a dyke across Treath Mawr, the estuary of the River Glaslyn, to shut out the sea further and carry a road linking Caernarvon and Merioneth. But during 1812 the sea threatened the unfinished dyke, money was running out and the project was in danger. Shelley at once promised to raise more money, at the same time offering to rent Madocks' house, Tan-yr-allt, perched in romantic isolation on the hillside above Tremadoc. Shelley's own arrest for debt in Caernarvon did not deter him; he was now accustomed to living on his future prospects and saw no reason why he should not raise money for others in the same way. The Caernarvon debt was soon settled; and he moved his party to London to find support for Madocks.

He found no one prepared to listen to his appeals. But there was something better to keep him in London, and this was the friendship of Godwin, who followed up his initial invitation to dinner with frequent meetings and lengthy talks on all aspects of Shelley's life. Godwin, now in his mid-fifties, lived very modestly with his second wife over their book shop in Skinner Street, Holborn; and here Shelley and Harriet came enthusiastically and often from their rooms in Lewis's Hotel, St James's.

The Godwin household was a genuinely extraordinary one. Godwin himself had risen from quite uneducated parents through the Dissenting academies to become the foremost philosopher of his age. In 1797 he married Mary Wollstonecraft, noted for her belief in women's rights and adherence to many of the doctrines of the French Revolution, much of which she witnessed at first hand. She had brought back from France a small daughter, Fanny, by an American businessman who had deserted her. When she died giving birth to Godwin's child, another Mary, he was left with the two tiny girls; he sought a second wife, and found a neighbour, Mary Jane Clairmont, with a small son and daughter of uncertain paternity; the two forlorn groups joined forces and in due course Mr and Mrs Godwin had a son.

So there were five children to be brought up: Fanny Imlay, who seems to have assumed she was Godwin's child and certainly called herself Fanny Godwin; Charles Clairmont, a bright and enterprising boy; Mary Godwin, the cleverest; Jane Clairmont, six months younger than Mary, dark, pretty and dramatic; and small William. Charles went to a local boys' school and was found a clerkship in a publishing firm; the girls were educated mostly at home. Reading was the habit of the whole family; money was always short; Mrs Godwin worked hard at organizing a children's book publishing firm. Godwin wrote and talked.

There is no doubt that, as well as welcoming a disciple, he saw in Shelley someone who would ease his perpetual financial problems.

In November 1812 Shelley met the eighteen-year-old Fanny, to whom he took a great liking, and Jane, who was a child of fourteen; Mary was away. As the Godwin friendship waxed, so poor Miss Hitchener's star waned. Harriet and Eliza Westbrook decided that she had erotic and financial designs on Shelley; he himself had suffered one of his intense revulsions, and took to calling her the Brown Demon and laughing at her behind her back. 'An artful, superficial, ugly, hermaphroditical beast of a woman' were his last words on her, and in November she was sent back to Sussex, bitterly aware that the warnings she had received from the worldly-wise were now justified, and for a while intent on pathetic attempts at vengeance. He apologized, as well he might, for his bad judgement and inconsistent behaviour, and prepared to pay her a small annuity, though there is no evidence that he ever did. Her departure was observed by Hogg, sought out by Shelley in his London chambers and drawn determinedly back into the fold. Hogg was unable to put aside his flirtatious manner with Harriet, although she had now achieved the dignity of pregnancy and was coolly cordial in return. A young poet who came into their circle in October, through Hookham, Thomas Love Peacock, was so impressed by Harriet's beauty and charm that he never lost his feeling for her and wrote her praises warmly long after her death. Certainly few brides would set themselves to learn Latin during their first pregnancy, as she did.

One further new friend was introduced to Shelley by Godwin, and this was John Newton, vegetarian and health fanatic; Shelley's own diet had been sparse since Oxford. Hogg complained bitterly about the food in his household, alleging that when he asked for pudding, Shelley answered 'a pudding is a prejudice'; and all who knew him agree that he lived largely on bread, raisins, honey, fruit and tea, and was quite regardless of meal-times. Vegetarianism was no hardship to him and for a while he saw it as a panacea; in *Queen Mab* he even predicts that the entire animal kingdom will become herbivorous.

His new friendships and enthusiasms had not swept the thought of Tremadoc from his mind. He returned with his household to Wales to take up residence at Tan-yr-allt, assist Madocks as far as possible, work on *Queen Mab* and embark on a course of reading under the guidance of Godwin. Plans were laid to invite Hogg and Hookham to stay in the spring. Shelley and Harriet seemed set for a happy winter, both full of a sense of purpose and

cheered by a friendly letter from his father in the
new year. But two political incidents disturbed him.
They were the hanging of some Yorkshiremen
convicted of machine-breaking, and the prison
sentences passed upon Leigh Hunt and his brother
for libelling the Prince Regent. Shelley suggested
to Hookham raising a subscription for the children
of the Luddites, and sent Leigh Hunt £20. Since
Shelley made no secret of his radical views, it is
possible that local disapproval of them lay behind
an incident that took place on the night of
26 February – possible, though far from certain.

On that day Dan Healy returned to them from
Barnstaple prison. The weather was stormy; about
eleven in the evening Shelley heard a noise from
his bedroom and went down with a pistol. He said
he saw a man leaving through a window, who fired
at him. After a struggle the man escaped, threat-
ening revenge on the whole family. Everyone in
the house now gathered in the parlour, but after a
while went back to bed; at about 4 a.m. the attacker
returned and again tried to shoot Shelley through
the window. Shelley's sketch of the man makes
him into a devil with horns. Some believe that the
incident was arranged to frighten him; others that
he hallucinated the whole affair; others again that
he engineered it in order to give himself an excuse
to leave the district. None of these explanations

substantially alters our picture of Shelley, since we know from other evidence that he did incur hostility for his political views; that he was subject to hallucinations; and that under stress he was not always trustworthy.

As fast as they could, the Shelleys left Wales and, as they had done after the similar incident at Keswick, sailed for Dublin, summoning Hogg to join them for a holiday. But before he could arrive they had moved on to see the lakes at Killarney; and here, slightly mysteriously, Shelley and Harriet left Eliza and Dan and returned to London, where they settled in Cook's Hotel, Albemarle Street, to await the birth of their child. Hogg came on after them, and presently Eliza and Dan made their way to London also. Shelley was now busy correcting *Queen Mab* and writing notes to it. The poem was dedicated to Harriet:

Whose is the love that gleaming through the world,
Wards off the poisonous arrow of its scorn?
    Whose is the warm and partial praise,
    Virtue's most sweet reward?

Beneath whose looks did my reviving soul
Riper in truth and virtuous daring grow?
    Whose eyes have I gazed fondly on,
    And loved mankind the more?

Harriet! on thine: – thou wert my purer mind;
Thou wert the inspiration of my song;
   Thine are these early wilding flowers,
   Though garlanded by me.

She explained to a friend that although the poem
was printed, 'it must not be published under pain
of death, because it is too much against every exist-
ing establishment'. It was true that Hookham
would not publish for fear of prosecution, but he
printed 250 copies at Shelley's expense, turning
down a volume of his short poems at the same
time. About seventy copies of *Queen Mab* were
privately distributed. Such was its reputation that,
in 1821, the cartoonist Cruikshank put a placard
announcing 'Queen Mab or Killing no Murder' at
the centre of a group of revolutionaries. Its popu-
larity developed only later, with radicals, for whom
it became an almost sacred text, appreciating it
primarily for its attitudes and arguments. *Queen
Mab* is one of the bizarre landmarks of our literature, a cross-breeding between two quite separate
traditions, that of the elaborate allegorical fairy-
tale and that of the historical and political polemic.
The fairy queen, the sleeping girl's spirit and the
magic car travelling away from the earth through
space make a disconcerting start to a disquisition
on the organization of society. Yet Shelley's attacks

are powerful and often memorably phrased as he reveals the horrors brought by monarchy, commerce and the enslavement of labour to maintain a class of 'drones' –

> . . . many faint with toil,
> That few may know the cares and woe of sloth.

On war, religion and marriage he is equally pungent. God is shown as a projection of man's pride and cruelty, organized religion as contributing to rather than reducing human suffering, the current view of marriage and chastity as encouragement to hideous hypocrisy. And sometimes his vision has the weird splendour of his contemporary, Goya:

> Even Time, the conqueror, fled thee in his fear;
> That hoary giant, who, in lonely pride,
> So long had ruled the world, that nations fell
> Beneath his silent footstep . . .

*Queen Mab* is over two thousand lines in length, written partly in blank verse and partly in free, unrhymed lyrical sections modelled on Southey's verse. Within its odd fairy convention it progresses straightforwardly enough from a picture of the world as an 'ant-hill' full of mistakes and miseries to a vision of an ideal future. And although Shelley regarded it as a very imperfect piece of work, he maintained the intellectual positions adopted in the text and in the remarkable and lucid prose notes.

While he was working on his text, Harriet was hoping that she might be allowed to give birth to her first child at Field Place. And with the approach of his majority Shelley wrote to his father seeking a reconciliation and regretting his 'Follies' (he also ordered a large carriage for his expanding family). His father replied, but when Shelley explained that his *opinions* had not changed at all, there was an end to the exchange. On 23 June a daughter, Eliza Ianthe, was born – not at Field Place, but at lodgings in Half Moon Street. Peacock visited the family and was touched by Shelley's attitude towards the baby: 'He was extremely fond of it, and would walk up and down a room with it in his arms for a long time together, singing to it a monotonous melody of his own making.' *To Ianthe*, the sonnet he wrote in September, also seems to express a blissful contentment with his new fatherhood:

> I love thee, Baby! for thine own sweet sake;
> Those azure eyes, that faintly dimpled cheek,
> Thy tender frame so eloquently weak,
> Love in the sternest heart of hate might wake;

But more, when o'er thy fitful slumber bending
Thy mother folds thee to her wakeful heart,
Whilst love and pity in her glances blending,
All that thy passive eyes can feel, impart;
More, when some feeble lineaments of her
Who bore thy weight beneath her spotless bosom,
As with deep love I read thy face, recur,
More dear art thou, O fair and fragile blossom,
Dearest, when most thy tender traits express
The image of thy Mother's loveliness. –

Yet from this time dissension appears between Shelley and Harriet, one reason being that she did not wish to carry out his passionate wish that she should feed the baby herself. To Harriet, Eliza began to seem her ally against Shelley; and to Shelley also.

The need for economies arose again. Dan was dismissed, and the family moved thirty miles out of London to Bracknell in Berkshire, a house called High Elms belonging to Mrs Newton's sister, a Mrs Boinville, who had just lost her husband in the Russian campaign. She and her eighteen-year-old daughter Cornelia lived near by and despite their mourning were warmly welcoming neighbours. Shelley was delighted with them; he also invited Peacock to stay. Peacock was seven years older than Shelley, an even better classical scholar and a fine writer; he shared some of Shelley's prankishness but in the long run proved his most reliable and level-headed friend. Discreet, humorous and kind: of all Shelley's circle, he is the most agreeable.

Bracknell was not far enough to protect Shelley from his London creditors. The coach was packed up, Peacock agreed to accompany the family, and Shelley found a money-lender ready to lend him £500, a post-obit loan payable on his grandfather's death at a rate of 300 per cent; it had become perforce his usual way of raising money. With this they set off, first for the Lakes and then, finding no house to let there, for Edinburgh again. They did not stay long; in November they were all back in Bracknell, where Shelley now made very little attempt to hide the fact that he found the company of both the Boinville ladies far more interesting than that of his wife and sister-in-law. For a short time he actually stayed in the Boinville house, taking Italian lessons with Cornelia.

> Thy dewy looks sink in my breast;
>   Thy gentle words stir poison there;
> Thou hast disturbed the only rest
>   That was the portion of despair!

He began an awkwardly phrased but perfectly explicit verse to her. He had earlier praised Harriet for her 'dewy' eyes also; but Harriet's dews of sympathy were for the moment dried. In March 1814 Shelley went through a second marriage ceremony with her, at St George's, Hanover Square, but this was either at her family's insistence or for technical reasons connected with raising money. She also conceived another child in March. None of this stopped her from departing with the baby Ianthe and Eliza, whom Shelley now held in abomination, for a holiday in the west country. It appears that Cornelia was removed from the scene, probably by an anxious fiancé, at the same time.

Attempts to explain Shelley's loss of love for Harriet, his own or anyone else's, tend to absurdity, since clever men can love stupid wives, unworldly men love wives who want new hats and smart clothes, short-tempered men put up with detested in-laws. Whatever Harriet's faults or virtues, Shelley was only twenty-one; what he had loved in her he loved no longer; for him, something had to change.

He fell into a state of severe dejection. 'I have sunk into a premature old age of exhaustion', he told Hogg. Mrs Boinville expressed the fear that Shelley's 'journeys after what he has never found, have racked his purse and his tranquillity'. One happy incident relieved this period. At the beginning of June Timothy Shelley was away from home, and Mrs Shelley persuaded him to make a secret visit to Field Place, his sisters and the servants entering into the conspiracy and Shelley agreeing to wear a military uniform as a disguise. The family chattered happily together in an untidy little sitting-room they called Confusion Hall; the scene, described by a family friend, is so bright and cheerful that the sense of what Shelley was losing is brought vividly home. Within another month he was to make that loss permanent and irreparable. A new band of sisters and a new set of family troubles were to take the ascendant.

# POCKET PENGUINS

# POCKET PENGUINS